Treasures

TONE POEMS FOR THE PIANO

by

Chris J Berry

authorHOUSE®

AuthorHouse™ UK Ltd.
500 Avebury Boulevard
Central Milton Keynes, MK9 2BE
www.authorhouse.co.uk
Phone: 08001974150

Published by AuthorHouse 8/07/2012

ISBN: 978-1-4772-2189-1 (sc)
ISBN: 978-1-4772-2190-7 (e)

Treasures

TONE POEMS FOR THE PIANO
by
Chris J Berry

CONTENTS

**This music book
is dedicated to Dolcie
on her 103rd birthday,
in gratitude for all the
guidance she gave us
as teenagers and
now today as
pensioners.**

Introduction

During the primary years, my sister and I were required to add a musical instrument to our education period; a requirement placed upon us by our parents. The choice of instrument was left to us; both choosing the piano, not from any careful consideration, simply because we had one. As far as I was concerned, five years of purgatory followed; aware of my contemporaries at play while I had to practice my pieces. After leaving school, mother's strategy had been realised— music being part of our lives by then.

Both my sister and I, having become reasonably competent pianists, the choice then was left to us to either continue on or do otherwise. Music, however, was very much an active past-time within our family circle; my aunt and uncle running a small dance band, skilfully arranging music for it themselves. Intrigued by their example, we joined some of our friends similarly interested. Our mother's wisdom of insisting we learned to play an instrument now came into its own, and we began to generate a repertoire as we moved out onto the teenage music scene.

Over the years, both of us have continued to enjoy music, my sister acquiring several keyboards, and myself a new piano. During a particularly traumatic period in my later life, I was grateful of my mother's fore-sight, immersing myself in music for relief. Throughout the nineteen nineties, I occupied myself in creating some tone poems that emulated the pets we had kept in the past. During this period, I was also involved in writing 'The Cyannian Trilogy', with another project on the horizon. In this fourth book, my autobiography Sixty Psychic Years, Mother encouraged me to dedicate a chapter to my tone poems. Her idea appealed to me, she suggesting that those who read the book it might help to reveal the purpose in all my writing, and the tone poems.

Undoubtedly, my tone poems will never make 'the Albert', but my hope is they will raise awareness that the wealth of a world is not measured by the minerals extracted from it. The content of the treasure chest, pictured on the front of my music album, represents what I consider to have been the real treasures that have graced my life. The pieces reflect the characters of our family pets and I sense their presence whenever I play them. Essentially, however, I feel the pieces could represent all pets, and raise nostalgic moments for their masters.

For me, it is the jingle of Tabby Sam's bell playing endlessly with her ball on a string; old Trampy, a gentle giant in every sense of the word; Bels, Mum's little miniature poodle, full of mischief, and who developed the ability to woof with the ball in her mouth so as not to lose it; Phoebe, a sedate and gracious old lady who honoured you by settling upon your lap; Poppy, Mum's little toy poodle, very bossy and definitely to be considered as number one. Last and by no means least, old Popsy. This piece raises many vivid memories in me: a dear, clever, tolerant little dog who bore the brunt of an unruly child's addresses for years. Pictured in the icon on the contents page, he still spans the years to wish me a happy birthday, courtesy of one of many pictures my father took of him.

But let us not forget Mother Earth. She remains the underlying purpose for all my submissions and prompts me to ask the question: will humanity, at last, realize how she has been abused before it is too late? Walking home from the hospital after an early mid-summer morning call-out, I was privileged to witness a Gossamer Sunrise: thousands of dew-ladened spider's webs on gorse bushes, set ablaze by the rising sun— sadly I had no camera. The picture used, however, reveals my part of Earth in all her majesty, and leaves me to deliberate on how we must all simply waltz in time with our world... CJB.

NOTES ON THE TONE POEMS

From the introduction, the reader will have undoubtedly realised my objective for writing these tone poems. These notes suggest ideas and methods on playing them, but as a guide only. Dynamics are scarce as it is my hope that a player's family pets may inspire them to apply their own interpretations.

Treasures: This title piece has been marked at a tempo of crochet = 152. The pedal settings, as in all the pieces, are, again, suggestions— left at the discretion of the player. The rallentando in bar 10 applies tenuto in the right hand with a softening staccato in the left hand, and then pauses on the chord at pianissimo (the pedal use here is optional). The first section starting at bar 31 is played with tenuto only, and then, as indicated, the repeat is played with tenuto and attack. Progressing to bar 60, the phrase is identical to that at bar 56 but introduces an attacked base theme, using discreet pedal to emphasise the sustained effect. From bar 64 a modest counterpoint theme is used where the melody is taken by a mid strand at tenuto, while maintaining an upper trill effect. A sensible balance is needed to avoid either section overpowering the other. The theme at bar 84 repeats the base section mentioned at bar 60. The finale at bar 95 can be played sensa tempo or a tempo, descending in staccato steps to pianissimo.

Tabby Samantha: Pedal ad lib. After the introduction at sensa tempo, bar 3 sets the tempo. At bar 4 the right hand represents the little cat's bell so needs to ring. The fingering over the descending thirds in bars 21, 22, 23 is a suggestion only. The key change to the tonic minor at bar 27 indicates sadness at the little cat's loss, and then back to the major key at bar 49 as she bounds off into the hereafter with her bell ringing. Again the fingering of the descending thirds at bars 68 and 69 is a suggestion only.

Trampy: Pedal ad lib. This piece is fairly straight forward, telling the story of a stout-hearted old plodder, as depicted in the left hand of the first section. In bar 17 the second section, the sweet nature of the old boy is revealed with the melody played at cantabile to a gentle chord accompaniment in the left hand. The finale, at sensa tempo bar 43, the left hand represents a flick of his tail, with the melody descending to its conclusion.

Bels: Pedal ad lib. In Bels, we imagine an impish little poodle daring you to take her ball. The left hand should not overpower the melody, so care is needed when using the pedal. The phrases at bars 9 to 15, 35 to 41, 59 to 67, represent her yaps with the final chord at bar 68 and 69 left to ring like a bell.

Phoebe: Pedal ad lib. This piece to be played cantabile with a gentle lilt. The phrases, beginning at bar 20 to 25, should be played without tempo and can be pulled and pushed for effect, returning to a tempo as indicated at bar 26. Similarly for bars 40 through to the finish pausing on a soft conclusion.

Gossamer Sunrise: Pedal ad lib. This piece, set at crochet = 130 should be played brightly. Depicting an early morning summers sunrise, it portrays Nature's beauty and drama. The runs in bar 119 particularly represent spiders rushing around in their webs in preparation for the days fly catch. A brief change from major to minor at bar 148 intercedes for the unfortunate fly, but then at bar 166 life goes on. The finale begins at bar 196 and descends to a pause in bar 200 with a simple statement in bar 203 concluding at pianissimo; note there is no pedal off sign after the last note— it is left to a fading ring.

The Simplicity Waltz: Pedal ad lib. Strict tempo is needed here, as the piece lends itself to those keen to waltz. A count is necessary at bars 3 and 5, 19 and 20, 36 and 37, 52 and 53, 69 and 70, 86 and 87 - 90 (with repeat), 104 and 105, 119 and 120, 125 and 126, 131 and 132. The finale at bar 133 ascends to pianissimo.

Poppy: Pedal ad lib. This piece requires a bit of study to achieve the results of a sweet, but complicated little dog, using an arpeggio theme in the left hand against runs in the right hand through bars 21 to 27. The left hand picks out accentuated descending notes through bars 73 to 80, placing a particular emphasis on the pause at bar 80. Leading up to the finale, beginning at bar 95, the piece reaches a crescendo, with a rallentando at bar 96 through 97, and then descending to pianissimo.

Popsy: pedal ad lib. This little dog is the aristocrat of them all, and his piece should be played with that in mind. Particular attention needs to be paid to pedal use, especially the sextuplets beginning at bar 20 through to 30— playing them at strict tempo, and in particular, the transition into the finale at bar 31.

It remains my hope that anyone playing these pieces shares my opinion that little souls like these are the true treasures of Earth. Written at a time when life was at a low ebb, they continue to raise nostalgic memories of the pets that have graced my life when I play them. It is my plan in the future to extract the midi files from the score, and make them available as a playing guide on my website for download.

TREASURES

Chris J Berry

Tabby Samantha

Chris J Berry

TRAMPY

Chris J Berry

BELS

Chris J Berry

PHOEBE

Chris J Berry

17

Gossamer Sunrise

Chris J Berry

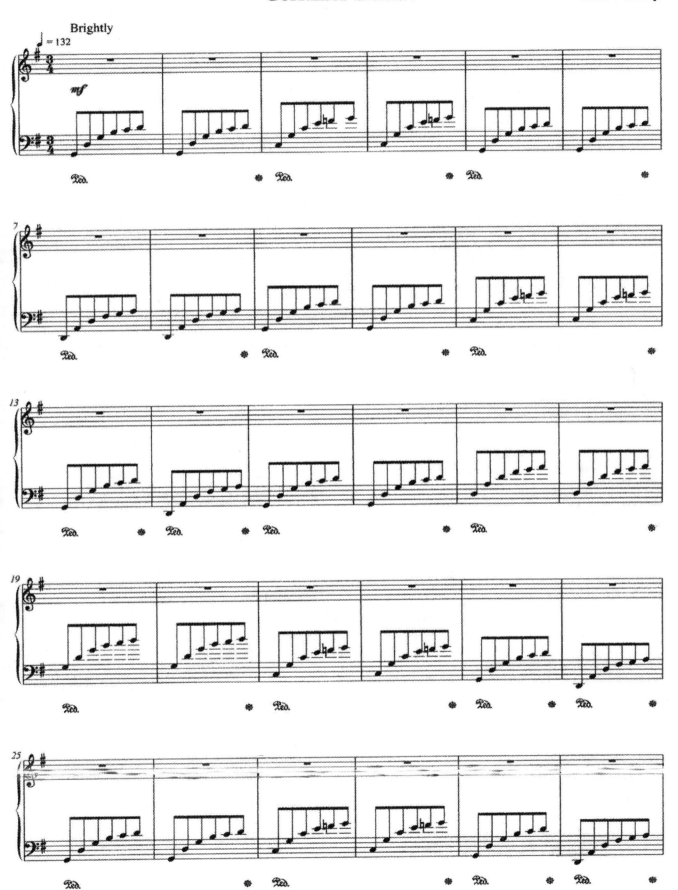

21

24

THE SIMPLICITY WALTZ

Chris J Berry

POPPY

Chris J Berry

33

POPSY

Chris J Berry

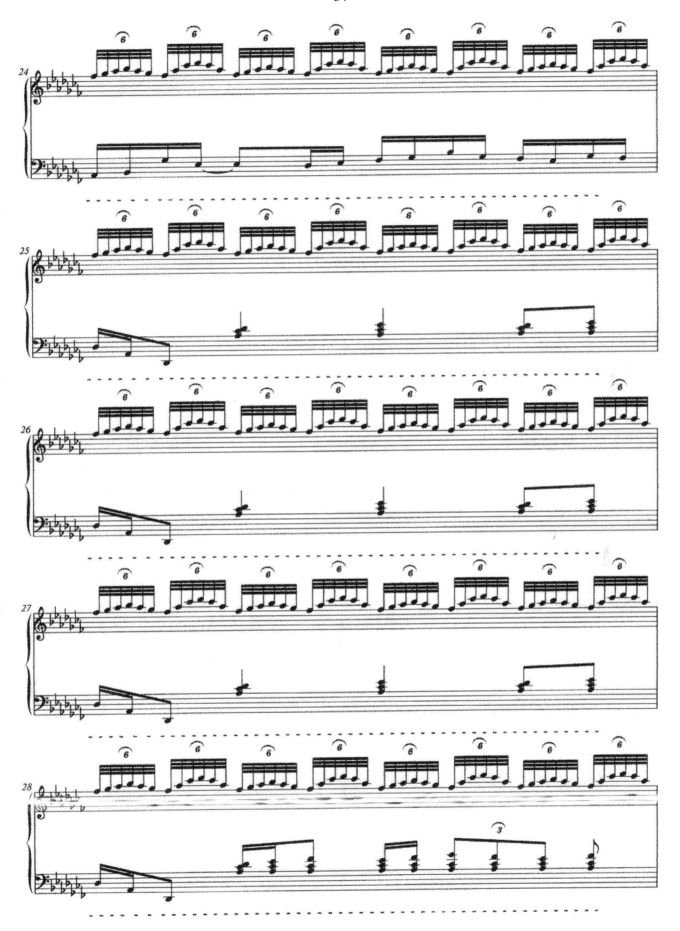

38

About the Author

***

Since writing the first of his books, it has always been the author's main objective to try and encourage others to help the creatures and people of our planet— this music album continuing in that quest. The first hand-written score appeared at a time when the author was suffering a particularly traumatic period in his life. Seeking a little respite in music, he became intrigued by his sister's music compositions and set about creating some of his own. Towards the end of the nineteen nineties he had completed six tone poems, going on to finish three more by the end of that decade. The impression he became aware of then, was to dedicate each one to a pet that had graced his life since childhood. Moving into the new millennia, he shelved the music project to complete the Cyannian Trilogy; the first book of which was published in July two thousand and six. The trilogy finished he began his autobiography, with the notion of dedicating a chapter describing the creation and purpose for writing the album. However, with the inspiration for a new series of books pressing him, the intention to attach his music to his autobiography proved unrealistic. In retrospect, and encouraged by other views, the music project stands on its own. Finally finished in the autumn of two thousand and eleven, the proofing of the album was completed for publication in the spring of two thousand and twelve.

***

Published Works by Chris J Berry

***

Cataclysm Earth - DJ - ISBN: 9781425946784

*

Cataclysm Earth - SC - ISBN: 9781425946791

*

Cataclysm Earth - ebook - ISBN: 9781452085708

***

Heritage from Cyan - DJ - ISBN: 9781434315076

*

Heritage from Cyan - SC - ISBN: 9781434315069

*

Heritage from Cyan - ebook - ISBN: 9781452069937

***

Avataria - DJ - ISBN: 9781434377494

*

Avataria - SC - ISBN: 9781434377487

*

Avataria - ebook - ISBN: 9781452083346

***

Poems of Petals, Poodles and Prayers
by Ivy Berry

SC - ISBN – 9781438938356

*

ebook - ISBN – 9781452089799
Compiled and Illustrated
by Chris J Berry

***

Sixty Psychic Years - DJ - ISBN: 9781452010397

*

Sixty Psychic Years - SC - ISBN: 9781452010380

*

Sixty Psychic Years - ebook - ISBN: 9781452022840

***

The Spiritual Inception – DJ – ISBN: 9781456779016

*

The Spiritual Inception – SC – ISBN: 9781456779009

*

The Spiritual Inception – ebook – ISBN: 9781456779023

***

A Rendezvous with Evil – DJ – ISBN: 9781468582758
*

A Rendezvous with Evil– SC – ISBN: 9781468582741
*

A Rendezvous with Evil – ebook – ISBN: 9781468582765
***

All titles available in
Amazon Kindle and
Google ebook format.
***

Chris J Berry
*

http://www.chrisjberry.co.uk
***

Acknowledgement
*

Scores arranged using Mozart Music Notation Software:
*

http://www.mozart.co.uk

***

Printed in the United States
By Bookmasters